WEATHER

Andrew Haslam & Barbara Taylor

Consultant: Tim Davie, Hydrologist
Queen Mary and Westfield College
University of London

World Book

in association with

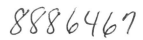

Published in the United States and Canada by
World Book, Inc.
525 W. Monroe Street
Chicago, IL 60661
in association with Two-Can Publishing Ltd.

Text: Barbara Taylor
Editor: Robert Sved
Art Director: Carole Orbell
Senior Designer: Gareth Dobson
Senior Managing Editor: Christine Morley
Production: Leila Peerun
Photography: John Englefield
Picture research: Lyndsey Price, Dipika Parmar Jenkins
Model-makers: Melanie Williams, Peter Griffiths
Art direction and model-making for experiments: Andrew Haslam
Special thanks to Sharon Nowakowski and Patricia Ohlenroth
Series concept and original design © Andrew Haslam

**For information on other World Book products, call 1-800-255-1750, x 2238,
or visit us at our Web site at http://www.worldbook.com.**

ISBN: 0-7166-5112-2 (hard cover)
ISBN: 0-7166-5113-0 (soft cover)

Haslam, Andrew.
    Weather / Andrew Haslam & Barbara Taylor.
        p.   cm. -- (Make-it-work!)
    Includes index.
    Summary: Clarifies the study of the forces and principles involved
with weather through the use of models and associated activities.
    ISBN 0-7166-5112-2. -- ISBN 0-7166-5113-0 (pbk.)
    1. Weather--Study and teaching--Juvenile literature. 2. Weather-
-Study and teaching--Activity programs--Juvenile literature.
I. Taylor, Barbara, 1954-   . II. Title. III. Series.
QC981.3.H37 1997
551.6--dc21   96-53572

Photographic credits:
Tony Stone Worldwide: p4(tr); Still Pictures: p5(tr); NASA: p8(tr); Zentrale Farbbild Agentur GmbH: p15(tl);
Doug Scott/Chris Bonington Library: p19(tl); Leonard Lee Rue/Science Photo Library: p28(tr);
Warren Faidley/Oxford Scientific Films: p32(tr); E.R. Degginger/Oxford Scientific Films: p34(tr);
B. Harris/Zentrale Farbbild Agentur GmbH: p41(tl); Still Pictures: p41(tr); Jules Cowan/Bruce Coleman Limited: p42(tr);
M. Nimmo/FLPA: p44(tl); Steve C. Kaufman/Bruce Coleman Limited: p45(tr).

Maps:
© The Meteorological Office, United Kingdom: p4(bl); © Scan-globe A/S edn. 1991: p13(b).

Printed in Hong Kong.
1 2 3 4 5 6 7 8 9 10 01 00 99 98 97

Contents

Words marked in **bold** in the text are explained here

Studying the weather

Geography helps us to understand what happened to the Earth in the past, how it is changing now, and what might happen to it in the future. Studying the weather is an important part of geography. This job is done by **meteorologists,** who study all the things that make up the weather, such as wind, rain, clouds, and sunshine. They do this by looking at the changes in the layer of gases that surrounds the Earth called the **atmosphere**.

△ The weather can affect the type of home we live in. These houses in Singapore are built on stilts to protect people from floods that may happen when it rains.

People and weather

Since earliest times, people's lives have been affected by the weather. Basic needs, such as growing food and finding shelter, have always been linked to the weather of a place. Nowadays, the weather still greatly influences our lives, from the clothes we wear and the homes we live in to the food we grow and the transportation and communication we use.

◁ Meteorologists use charts like these to help them to predict the weather. You can use a camera, **thermometer,** and notebook to keep weather records.

Forecasting through the ages

People who can forecast the weather have always been important to society. During the Middle Ages, people made weather predictions based on the positions of stars and planets. Today, weather forecasters use new technology, such as **satellites** and huge computers. But anyone can begin to forecast the weather by taking a few measurements and looking at the clouds.

Make it Work!

The Make it Work! way of looking at geography is to carry out experiments and make things that help you to understand how geography shapes the world in which we live. By studying the models and following the step-by-step instructions, you will discover more about how the weather works.

Using this book

Meteorologists study a wide range of geographical subjects. Throughout this book, we have used symbols to show where information relates to particular topics. The symbols are:

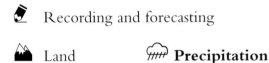

Recording and forecasting

Land   **Precipitation**

Temperature   Air and wind

▷ *Weather satellites give us very clear pictures of the moving layer of clouds that lies above the surface of the Earth.*

Recording the weather

It can be expensive to buy instruments to record the weather. This book shows you how to make simple models that can detect and measure changes in the weather.

▽ *The models in this book have arrows of different colors to show how air, water, and heat move around to make our weather.*

Safety

You may need to use sharp tools for some of the experiments in this book. Ask an adult to help you. Some of the weather measurements have to be taken outdoors. Be careful in wet, windy, icy, or stormy weather.

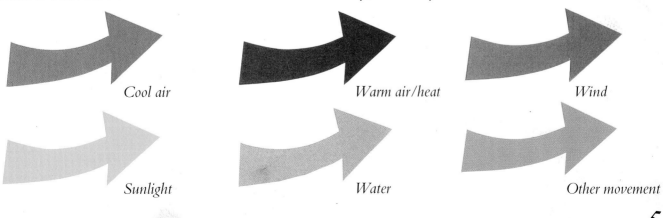

Cool air   *Warm air/heat*   *Wind*

Sunlight   *Water*   *Other movement*

Weather around the world

The weather is different all over the world. In some places it's always warm and in others it's freezing cold. Some areas have violent, stormy weather while others have calm, mild weather. When we ask about the weather, we usually want to know how wet it is (rainfall), and how hot it is (temperature).

▷ *This map shows the annual rainfall and temperature ranges of places all around the world. It also tells us where violent storms most frequently happen.*

🌧 Rainfall

The highest amount of rainfall over one year is near the **equator**, where more than 79 inches (2,000 millimeters) of rain falls in a year. Areas just north or south of the equator, such as North Africa or Australia, are mostly very dry. Places farther away from the equator, such as Europe, have plenty of rain. In the Arctic and Antarctica, there is little rain and most of it falls as snow.

🌡 Temperature

Temperatures are highest at the equator and gradually decrease toward the Arctic and Antarctica. Some places, especially those near the equator, such as Singapore, have an even temperature all year around. Places farther away from the equator, such as Paris and Montreal, have warm summers and cold winters. Temperature is measured in degrees Fahrenheit (°F) or degrees Celsius (°C).

The Arctic

North America

New Orleans, United States: 50 °F to 90 °F (10 °C to 32 °C)

Montreal, Canada: 5 °F to 77 °F (-15 °C to 25 °C)

▽ *This key explains the colors and symbols on the map.*

more than 6 inches (1,500 mm) of rain
4-6 inches (1,000-1,500 mm)
2-4 inches (500-1,000 mm)
1-2 inches (250-500 mm)
less than 1 inch (250 mm)

Rio de Janeiro, Brazil: 64 °F to 86 °F (18 °C to 30 °C)

South America

Hurricane

Tornado

Monsoon

Temperature reading for city

6

Paris, France:
32 °F to 75 °F
(0 °C to 24 °C)

Europe

Moscow, Russia:
10 °F to 77 °F
(-12 °C to 25 °C)

Irkutsk, Russia:
-15 °F to 75 °F
(-26 °C to 24 °C)

Asia

Tokyo, Japan:
36 °F to 86 °F
(2 °C to 30 °C)

Dalol, Ethiopia:
world's hottest average
temperature, 94 °F
(34.5 °C)

Bahrain:
57 °F to 100 °F
(14 °C to 38 °C)

Africa

Equator

Singapore:
75 °F to 86 °F
(24 °C to 30 °C)

Australia

Johannesburg, South Africa:
41 °F to 73 °F (5 °C to 23 °C)

⛆ ⚑ Special weather

Some weather features, such as violent
storms called **hurricanes** and **tornadoes**,
occur in only a few places around the world.
Monsoons, which bring long periods of
heavy rain, happen in some places near the
equator, such as Southeast Asia.

Sydney, Australia:
50 °F to 73 °F
(10 °C to 23 °C)

Vostok, Antarctica:
world's coldest average
temperature, -72 °F
(-58 °C)

Antarctica

The atmosphere

The Earth is wrapped in a layer of air, which is the mixture of gases we breathe. We call this layer the atmosphere. The atmosphere is thick near the surface of the Earth, where it is easy to breathe, but becomes thinner farther away from the Earth. About 560 miles (900 kilometers) away from the Earth, there is no more air left, only space. The weather only happens in the lowest part of the atmosphere.

△ *Seen from space, the atmosphere looks like a glowing, thin blue layer around the Earth.*

⚑ A mixture of gases

The atmosphere is made up of many gases. More than three-quarters of the atmosphere is nitrogen. About a fifth is oxygen, the gas that all living things need to stay alive. Other gases help keep out the sun's harmful rays, and some keep the Earth's heat in at night.

⚑ Layers in the atmosphere

The atmosphere is divided into five layers according to temperature. There are no solid boundaries between each layer – they fade into one another. The weather happens in the lowest layer, called the **troposphere**. This layer contains the water needed to make clouds.

TEST THE ATMOSPHERE

You will need: modeling clay, a candle, matches, a shallow bowl, a tall glass, colored water

1 Attach a candle to the center of a bowl using a lump of modeling clay. Pour water into the bowl, as shown above, and with an adult's help, light the candle.

2 With an adult's help, place the glass over the candle so that no air can enter.

Result: As fire needs oxygen to burn, the candle flame will go out when all the oxygen has disappeared. The water rises about one-fifth of the way up the glass, replacing the oxygen. This shows us that about one-fifth of our atmosphere is oxygen.

⚐ The lower atmosphere

The troposphere stretches about 6 miles (10 km) from the surface of the Earth. The next layer up is called the stratosphere. Fast aircraft fly here because the air is calmer than in the troposphere. The stratosphere includes a layer of a gas called **ozone**. This blocks out most of the sun's harmful rays that can make our skin burn. In the mesosphere, the coldest part of the atmosphere, temperatures fall to –148 °F (–100 °C).

⚐ The upper atmosphere

Above the mesosphere lies the thermosphere, the hottest layer. High temperatures burn up all the debris, such as meteors and old satellites, falling toward the Earth. In this layer, gases collide with sunlight and make bright splashes of light called auroras. These can sometimes be seen from the Earth's surface. The top layer of the atmosphere is called the exosphere. Some satellites circle the Earth in the exosphere, but most are out in space.

▽ *This model shows the five layers of the atmosphere. You can also see some features of each layer.*

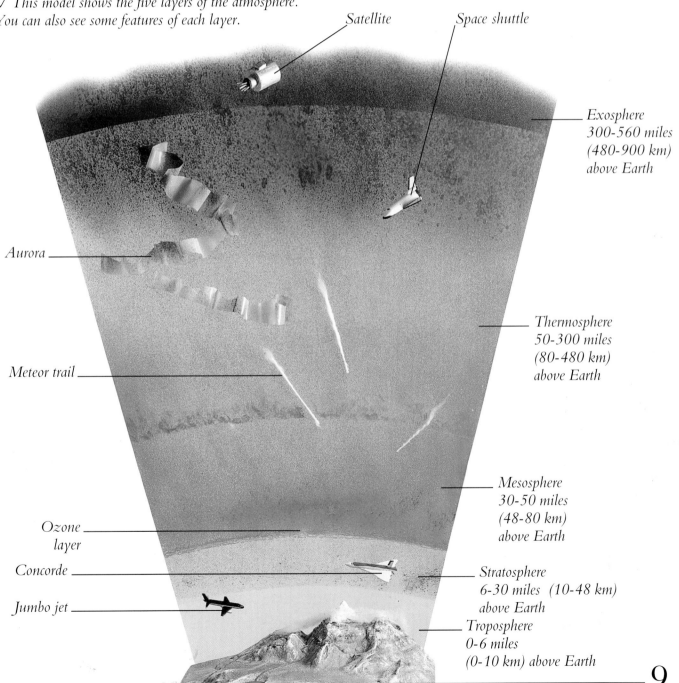

Satellite

Space shuttle

Exosphere
300-560 miles
(480-900 km)
above Earth

Aurora

Thermosphere
50-300 miles
(80-480 km)
above Earth

Meteor trail

Mesosphere
30-50 miles
(48-80 km)
above Earth

Ozone
layer

Stratosphere
6-30 miles (10-48 km)
above Earth

Concorde

Jumbo jet

Troposphere
0-6 miles
(0-10 km) above Earth

Making the weather

Three things are needed to make the weather: water, air, and heat. The sun's heat stirs up the atmosphere, making the air move. The moving air becomes wind, which carries heat and water around the Earth. This makes the weather happen.

▽ *This model shows the sun, wind, and rain in action on the surface of the Earth.*

🌧 **Water in the air**

When the sun heats up oceans, rivers, lakes, and plants, the atmosphere soaks up water from them like a sponge. The water turns into an invisible gas called **water vapor**, which stays in the air. Water vapor is a small but important part of the air. When the air cools down, the water vapor turns back into drops of liquid water again, forming clouds and rain.

🚩 **Air on the move**

When air around the Earth cools down or warms up, it moves. Warm air is lighter than cool air and it rises. Cool air is heavier and it sinks. Air rising and sinking causes winds all over the world, from such small winds as sea breezes to larger winds that circle the globe.

Water droplets collect in clouds.

Air rising and sinking causes the wind to blow.

The sun's rays heat the ground which warms the air.

Water falls to the Earth's surface as rain.

☿ The sun's rays

The sun sends out **energy** in the form of light and heat. As this energy enters the Earth's atmosphere, some of it is absorbed or scattered by gases. Further down, in the troposphere, clouds reflect more energy back into space. Only about half of the energy that reaches the atmosphere passes through it to heat the Earth's surface.

▷ *This model shows how the sun's rays lose energy as they pass through the atmosphere.*

☿ Heating the air

Although the sun's heat warms the air, it does not do so directly. The sun heats the ground or the sea, and the warm surface then heats the air from below. A radiometer is used to measure the energy given off by the warm air.

MAKE A RADIOMETER

You will need: a glass jar with lid, cardboard, aluminum foil, a matchstick, black paper, thread, glue, tape

Energy from the sun

7% is scattered by the atmosphere

16% is absorbed by gases in the atmosphere

23% is reflected by clouds

3% is absorbed by clouds

47% is absorbed by the Earth's surface

4% is reflected by land and oceans

1 Cut four 1-inch (2-centimeter) squares of cardboard. Cover both sides of two squares with black paper and two with foil.

2 Glue the squares to the matchstick, as shown above. The silver squares should be at right angles to each other, as should the black squares.

3 Tape one end of the thread to the end of the matchstick. Tape the other end of the thread to the middle of the inside of the lid. Put the lid on the jar and make sure that the cardboard cross can spin inside the jar.

4 On different days, place your radiometer outside in the sunshine and note how often the cross spins in one minute.

Result: When the jar warms up, the black squares heat up more easily than the silver squares. Hot air bounces off the black squares and pushes the cross around. The cross spins more quickly when there is more sunshine.

Heat and climate

Climate is the pattern of weather for a place. This pattern is roughly the same each year. Some places have warm climates, some have cold climates, and some have medium, or **temperate**, climates. The climate of a place depends mainly on its distance from the equator. It is hottest at the equator and becomes colder toward the **poles**.

▷ *This map shows the main climate zones of the world.*

⚡ Curved Earth

The Earth's surface is curved. This is why different parts of the Earth receive different amounts of heat from the sun. At the equator, the sun's rays hit the Earth directly. The sun is overhead at midday and its rays are concentrated on a small area. This makes areas around the equator very hot. At all other places, the sun's rays hit the Earth less directly.

▽ *This model shows how the sun's rays strike the Earth directly at the equator but are more spread out at the poles.*

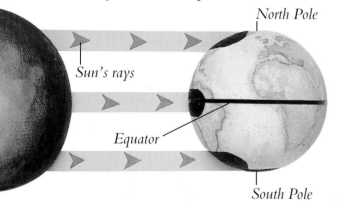

Sun's rays

Equator

North Pole

South Pole

▽ *This key explains the colored areas of the map.*

■ Tropical

■ Subtropical

□ Dry

■ Warm temperate

■ Cool temperate

■ Mountain and polar

⚡ The cold poles

At the poles, the heat from the sun's rays is spread over a wide area, so the ground cannot warm up quickly. Here, the sun is always low in the sky, even at midday. The sun's rays also travel farther to reach the poles than to reach the equator. This means they lose more of their heating power.

⚡ ⛰ Mountains and coasts

Climate is also affected by how high a place is and how near the coast it is. The higher up a place is, the colder its climate will be. On mountains, it is possible to move through different climates as you climb from the base toward the snowy peaks. The climate of coastal places is affected by the temperature of sea water near the coast.

Equator

♨ Climate zones

The Earth's climate can be divided into six main zones. These range from hot **tropical** and **subtropical** climates at the equator to cold polar climates at the top and bottom of the Earth. The middle zones between the poles and the equator have temperate climates. Nearly half of the world's people live in these areas.

HEATING THE EARTH

You will need: a flashlight, a globe, cardboard, scissors, a large coin

1 Place a coin on a piece of cardboard. Draw around it and cut out the circle.

2 Shine a flashlight toward the globe through the hole in the cardboard.

3 Move the cardboard to direct a circle of light at the equator.

Sunlight at the equator

4 Keep the flashlight still and move the cardboard up to shine light at the North Pole.

Sunlight at the North Pole

Result: The light makes a small, bright dot at the equator but is paler and more spread out at the poles.

The seasons

In most parts of the world, the weather changes during the year. Each time of year with a particular kind of weather is called a **season**. Temperate areas have four seasons: spring, summer, autumn, and winter. Seasons happen because the Earth tilts at an angle as it goes around the sun.

Warm and cold

The Earth moves around the sun once a year. As it moves, places are tipped closer to the sun to make warm seasons and farther away from the sun to make cold seasons. Seasons are opposite in the Northern and Southern **hemispheres**.

▽ *This model shows how the Earth's journey around the sun produces the seasons.*

Changing seasons

1. From June to August, as shown below, the North Pole is nearer the sun than the South Pole. It is summer in the north and winter in the south.
2. From September to November, the North Pole starts to move away from the sun. This brings autumn in the north and spring in the south.
3. From December to February, the South Pole is nearer the sun, bringing summer in the south and winter in the north.
4. From March to May, the North Pole starts to move back toward the sun. It is then spring in the north and autumn in the south.

Photographs on the next page show how this temperate region changes during the year.

4. March to May

This arrow shows the direction in which the Earth spins.

North Pole

Sun

3. December to February

1. June to August

South Pole

These arrows show the Earth's movement around the sun.

2. September to November

14

▽ *These photographs show the seasons in Connecticut, marked as a red square on the model left.*

1 *Summer*

2 *Autumn*

3 *Winter*

4 *Spring*

Polar seasons

Areas close to the poles are tilted nearer to the sun and farther away from the sun than other parts of the Earth. They have only two seasons – six months of summer followed by six months of winter. As the sun never sets in summer, these areas are sometimes called *lands of the midnight sun.*

Tropical seasons

In tropical areas, near the equator, the sun's rays always hit the Earth directly, and the tilt of the Earth does not affect the weather much. It feels warm all year around. Although the temperature changes very little, some areas have wetter climates than others.

Wet and dry seasons

In some tropical areas, especially in southern Asia, there are wet and dry seasons. These are caused by winds changing direction. In the summer monsoon season, the winds blow off the sea, bringing rain and floods. In the winter, they blow off the dry land, causing a hot dry season.

WATCH THE SEASONS

You will need: a light bulb in a standing light socket, a rubber ball, pieces of ¼-inch (5-mm) and ½-inch (10-mm) dowel, two squares of soft wood, a drill, a bradawl, paints, glue

1 Make a model Earth by painting a map of the world on the rubber ball. With an adult's help, use a bradawl to poke a hole into the North and South poles. Push the ¼-inch dowel through the Earth.

2 With an adult's help, drill a ½-inch hole in the center of one square of wood. Push the ½-inch dowel into the square. Glue the Earth to the dowel so that it is tilted.

3 Set up the Earth and sun—the light bulb—on a square of wood, as shown.

4 Move the Earth around the sun to see how the position of the Earth changes during each season.

△ *Summer in north, winter in south*   △ *Winter in north, summer in south*

Air temperature

The temperature of the air around you makes you feel hot or cold. Air temperature is affected by the climate and the season. It also depends on the time of day. Our days and nights happen because the Earth spins once every 24 hours. As it spins, the Earth receives different amounts of heat from the sun.

🌡 Thermometers

Thermometers are used to measure temperature. They are usually made with a narrow tube containing mercury or alcohol. These liquids expand when they warm up and contract when they cool down. So, as the temperature rises, the liquid moves up the tube.

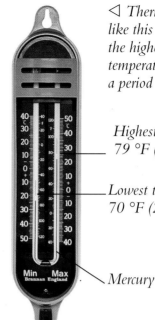

◁ *Thermometers like this one record the highest and lowest temperature over a period of time.*

Highest temperature 79 °F (26 °C)

Lowest temperature 70 °F (20 °C)

Mercury

MAKE A WATER THERMOMETER

You will need: a glass bottle, colored water, a jug, a rubber stopper with a hole, rubber bands, modeling clay, a stick, scissors, cardboard, tape, a clear plastic tube, pens, an ice bucket and ice, glue

1 Push the tube into the stopper and seal any gaps with modeling clay.

2 Mark ½-inch (1-cm) divisions on a strip of cardboard and glue it to the stick. Fix the stick behind the bottle using rubber bands.

3 Using the jug, fill the bottle with water up to the brim. Plug in the stopper so that the water rises about halfway up the tube. Tape the tube in place to complete your thermometer.

4 Place the thermometer in an ice bucket. Fill the bucket with ice cubes.

5 Water expands when it gets warmer and contracts when it gets colder. So the water level falls as it gets colder. Cut a small triangle out of the cardboard. After about 10 minutes, mark the water level with the triangle. This is zero on your scale.

6 Take the thermometer out of the bucket and leave it outside in the shade. Wait for the water level to rise and count the divisions from zero. Make a note of this temperature.

7 Let the thermometer sit a day and take the temperature once again. Has it gotten warmer or colder?

⬆ Warming up

The sun's energy heats the land during the day. The air around the Earth takes time to warm up, so the warmest time of day is usually in the middle of the afternoon, not at noon when the Earth receives the most energy.

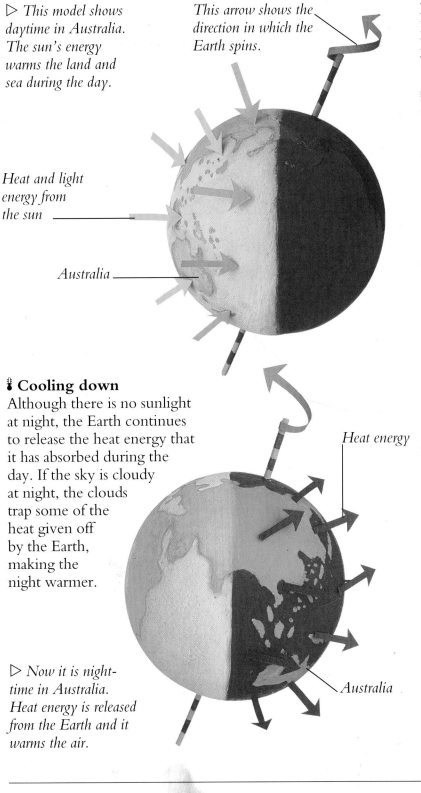

▷ *This model shows daytime in Australia. The sun's energy warms the land and sea during the day.*

This arrow shows the direction in which the Earth spins.

Heat and light energy from the sun

Australia

⬆ Cooling down

Although there is no sunlight at night, the Earth continues to release the heat energy that it has absorbed during the day. If the sky is cloudy at night, the clouds trap some of the heat given off by the Earth, making the night warmer.

Heat energy

Australia

▷ *Now it is night-time in Australia. Heat energy is released from the Earth and it warms the air.*

⬆ ⛰ Absorb or reflect?

Air temperatures near the Earth's surface depend on the temperature of the land beneath. Different surfaces absorb different amounts of heat. Snow reflects the sun's rays and absorbs very little heat, so the air above it stays cool. However, sand in the desert absorbs heat more easily, so the air above it becomes warmer.

⬆ 🚩 Wind chill

Your body gives off heat, making a thin layer of warm air around you. But if the wind blows away this warm air faster than your body can replace it, you feel cold, even on a warm day. This is called wind chill.

HEATING LAND

You will need:
sugar, sand, two small thermometers, two dishes, a lamp

1 Fill one dish with sugar and the other with sand. Place a thermometer into each dish.

2 Shine a lamp on the dishes. The thermometer readings will rise. Which rises faster?

Result: The sand warms up more quickly than the sugar. This shows that some materials can absorb heat more easily than others.

Air pressure

The weight of the air pressing down on the Earth is called air pressure. Although you don't notice it, the air around you does not always weigh the same. When the air is heavy, it presses down hard and makes high pressure. This usually brings good weather. When the air is light, there is low pressure, which usually brings clouds and rain.

⚑ Warm and cool air

Air pressure varies from place to place. This is mainly because the air temperature is always changing. When air is warm, it is light and rises, leaving behind an area of low pressure (see below). When air is cool, it is heavy so it sinks, making an area of high pressure (see right).

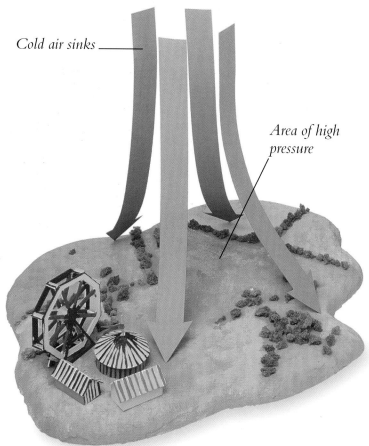

Cold air sinks

Area of high pressure

△ *This model shows cold air sinking, forming an area of high pressure.*

⚑ Pressure and rain

In areas of low pressure, rising warm air starts to cool down. When warm air gets cooler, the water vapor in the air **condenses** and becomes liquid water. This is why there is often rain in low pressure areas. In an area of high pressure, air sinks and starts to warm up. Warm air can hold a large amount of water vapor without making rain, so areas of high air pressure usually have clear, dry weather.

⚑ Pressure and the wind

The atmosphere is always working to balance areas of pressure. So air moves into areas of low pressure from surrounding areas of high pressure. This movement of air creates the wind. Strong winds happen if there is a big pressure difference between two areas.

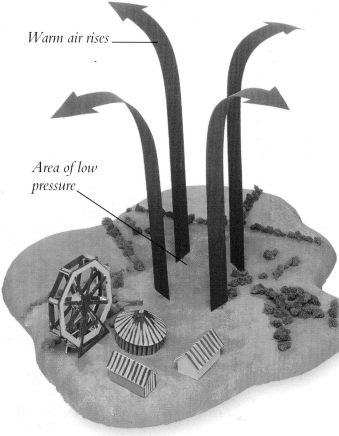

Warm air rises

Area of low pressure

△ *This model shows warm air rising, forming an area of low pressure.*

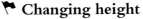 **Changing height**
Air pressure decreases as you rise. This is because there is less air pushing down on the Earth's surface at higher levels, such as a mountaintop. Air pressure is measured with a **barometer**, in units called millibars.

◁ *High up in the mountains, the air pressure is low, so the air is light and contains little oxygen. Climbers may carry oxygen tanks with them to help them breathe.*

 Feeling air pressure
If you travel by plane, you may feel a change in air pressure when your ears pop. The air pressure inside your ears is higher than in the plane and it pushes your eardrums out. As you swallow, the air pressure inside your ears goes down and your eardrums "pop" back into place.

MAKE A BAROMETER

You will need: a glass bottle, a bowl, cardboard, colored water, glue, pens, scissors

1 Fill the bottle with the colored water. Place the empty bowl over the bottle and carefully turn them upside down. Make sure the bottle is standing securely on its neck before letting go.

2 Gently let some water out of the bottle until it is about two-thirds full.

3 Draw very small divisions on a piece of cardboard and glue the cardboard on the bottle. Cut out a small triangle and glue it on the cardboard to mark the level of the water, as shown below left.

4 Leave your barometer in the shade. Make a note of how much the water level rises or falls each day.

▽ *Here the barometer shows that the air pressure has dropped.*

Result: When there is high air pressure, the air pushes down on the water in the bowl. This makes the water level rise in the bottle. The higher the level, the higher the air pressure.

Air on the move

Wind is moving air. Air always moves from an area of high pressure to an area of low pressure. Winds that blow around the world are called global winds. Smaller winds, that may happen near coasts or mountains, are called local winds.

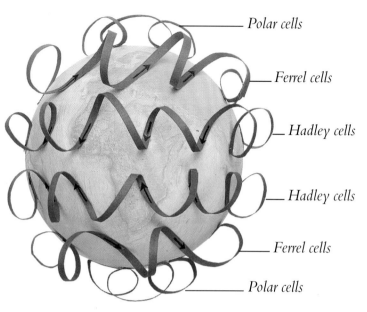

Polar cells

Ferrel cells

Hadley cells

Hadley cells

Ferrel cells

Polar cells

⚑ Global winds

In each hemisphere, there are three circles of wind, called cells, as shown right. At the equator, warm air rises and begins to move toward the poles. The air cools, sinks, and moves back toward the equator, forming Hadley cells. At the poles, cold air sinks. As the air moves away from the poles, it warms up and rises, forming polar cells. The middle cells, called Ferrel cells, are pushed around by the moving air to either side of them.

△ *This model shows the huge patterns of global winds that snake around the world.*

▷ *This model shows the directions of the world's prevailing winds.*

Polar easterlies

Prevailing westerlies

Trade winds

Equator

Trade winds

Prevailing westerlies

Polar easterlies

⚑ Prevailing winds

The spiraling cells create winds on the Earth's surface that blow mainly from one direction. These are called prevailing winds. Prevailing winds that blow toward the equator are called trade winds because they were used by sailing ships carrying goods to trade around the world. In temperate areas, there are winds from the west called prevailing westerlies. In polar areas, there are winds from the east called polar easterlies.

⚑ Why do winds spiral?

If the Earth did not spin, all the winds would blow directly from north to south or south to north. Instead, winds are dragged sideways by the spin of the Earth. This is called the **Coriolis effect**. It makes winds bend to the right in the Northern Hemisphere and to the left in the Southern Hemisphere.

MAKE A WEATHER VANE

You will need: Some ½-inch and ¼-inch (12-mm and 5-mm) dowel, cardboard, tape, a push pin, a compass, a bead, a drill, scissors, colored pens

1 With an adult's help, drill two ¼-inch holes, at right angles, through a long piece of ½-inch dowel. Push two dowels through these holes to make a cross.

2 For the vane, ask an adult to help you drill a small hole through the halfway point of a ¼-inch dowel.

3 Stick the pin through the ¼-inch dowel and bead, as shown right, and push it into the top of the larger dowel.

4 Cut out pieces of cardboard and color them, as shown. Tape them to the ends of the dowels.

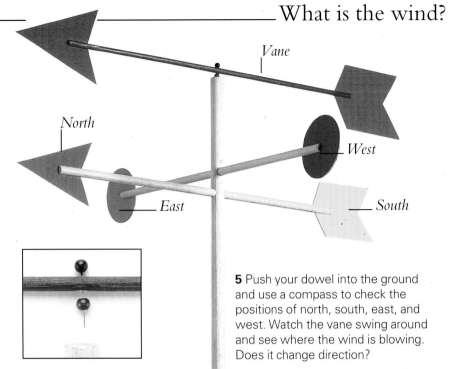

5 Push your dowel into the ground and use a compass to check the positions of north, south, east, and west. Watch the vane swing around and see where the wind is blowing. Does it change direction?

🏴 **Sea breezes**

Local winds that happen at the coasts are called land and sea breezes. During the day, the land heats up faster than the sea, so warm air rises off the land and a cool breeze is sucked in from the sea. This breeze replaces the rising warm air.

▷ *Sea breezes occur during the day when land is warmer than the sea.*

Warm air rises over the land.

Colder air rushes in from the sea.

🏴 **Land breezes**

During the night, the land cools down faster than the sea, so warm air rises over the sea and cool air sinks over the land. Cold air from the land is drawn out to the sea to replace the rising warm air. This creates a breeze blowing from the land to the sea.

▷ *Land breezes occur at night when the sea is warmer than the land.*

Colder air rushes away from the land.

Warm air rises over the sea.

Wind speed

The speed of the wind depends on the difference in air pressure between two areas. A slight difference produces a gentle breeze. A huge difference can cause a violent wind, such as a gale or a hurricane. Wind speed is measured with an instrument called an **anemometer**.

Breeze to hurricane

In 1805, Francis Beaufort, an admiral in the British Navy, invented a scale to measure the speed of the wind. It described the effect of the wind on ships and waves. This scale, called the Beaufort scale, has been adapted for use on land. The scale goes from zero (calm) to 17 (hurricane force) and shows how different wind speeds affect people and their surroundings. On the models below, the 13 commonly used stages of the Beaufort scale have been grouped into six stages.

The Beaufort scale

Force 0-2
These are light winds that blow up to 7 miles per hour (11 kilometers per hour). Smoke rises or drifts gently and leaves rustle.

Force 3-4
These are gentle breezes that blow at 8-18 mph (12-28 kph). Small branches move and flags flap. Dust and paper blow about.

Force 7-8
These are gales that blow at 32-46 mph (50-74 kph). Twigs break off trees and whole trees may sway. It is hard to walk against the wind.

Force 9-10
These are strong gales that blow at 47-63 mph (75-102 kph). Branches break off trees and there may be slight damage to houses.

☃ ☄ Mapping the wind

On weather maps (see page 38), symbols tell us about the wind. A long pointer shows wind direction, and lines on the pointer show different wind speeds, based on the Beaufort scale.

0   1   2   3   4   5   6   7   8   9   10   11   12

△ *These symbols are used on maps to show the different forces of the Beaufort scale.*

Force 5-6

These are strong breezes that blow at 19-31 mph (29-49 kph). Small trees sway and there are small waves on lakes. It is also hard to use an umbrella.

Force 11-12

These are violent storms, such as hurricanes, that blow above 64 mph (103 kph). There may be widespread damage to buildings and the landscape.

MAKE AN ANEMOMETER

You will need: three pieces of corrugated cardboard [(two 5 inch (12 cm) x 8 inch (20 cm), one 3 ½ inch (9 cm) x 3 inch (7 cm)], colored paper, two 4 inch (10 cm) x 8 inch (20 cm) wooden blocks, thumb tacks, a wooden skewer, a straw, a drawing compass, a matchstick, a utility knife, glue, a pen

1 Glue colored paper to one side of each piece of cardboard. With the skewer, poke a hole through a corner of each large piece of cardboard 1 inch (2 cm) from each edge, as shown above.

2 Use a compass to draw two arcs on each of these pieces, one 3 inches (7 cm) from the hole and the other 2 ¾ inches (6.5 cm) away. With an adult's help, cut out these curved slots with a utility knife, as shown above. Mark equal divisions along these slots.

3 Glue the box together. Glue the straw to the long edge of the small piece of cardboard and push a matchstick into the short edge, as shown above.

4 Place the cardboard in position so that you can push the skewer through the holes and the straw, so that the cardboard hangs in place. Secure with pins, making sure that the matchstick pokes through one slot. Glue a paper triangle to the end of the matchstick.

5 Now point the flap towards the wind to measure its strength. Try measuring wind speed in different places outside. Does it vary?

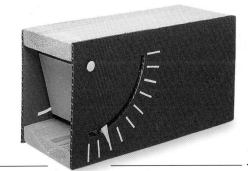

The water cycle

Water moves up into the sky and back down to the ground in a never-ending cycle called the water cycle. To do this, water has to change from liquid water on the ground into an invisible gas called water vapor. This process is called **evaporation**. Up in the sky, water vapor changes back into liquid water again. This process is called condensation.

▽ *On this model of the water cycle, blue arrows show the movement of water. Green arrows show how clouds move, often carrying rain toward the land.*

Clouding over
It is the sun's heat that makes liquid water on the Earth evaporate and mix with the air. As the air moves higher up in the sky, it cools down because temperatures are cooler higher up. Cool air cannot hold as much water vapor as warm air, so some of this water vapor condenses into droplets of water or freezes into tiny ice crystals. These gather together to make clouds.

Rainfall
When clouds cool down, rain may fall and collect in rivers, lakes, and oceans. Water also soaks into the soil and is taken in by plants and animals. When the sun heats the ground, the water evaporates and the cycle begins again. The amount of water on Earth always stays the same as it is continually moving through this cycle.

Water droplets collect together to make clouds.

Rain falls from clouds.

Water evaporates from the Earth's surface.

Water evaporates from the sea.

RECORD EVAPORATION

You will need: a white saucer, a crayon, colored water

1 Pour colored water into a saucer. With a crayon, draw a line on the saucer along the surface of the water.

2 Now leave your saucer in a warm place for a day.

Result: A lot of the water evaporates and the water level drops. Leave your saucer in a cool place. Does the level fall farther in warm or cold conditions?

Wind blows air from place to place, so water evaporating in one place falls as rain in another.

Rain falls from clouds.

Water flows along rivers to the sea.

Water seeps through rocks to the sea.

Water and heat

When water evaporates, it takes in heat, and when it condenses, it gives off heat. So as water in the water cycle is moved around the world, heat also moves. This changes the weather, because heat makes the air move and the movement of air makes the weather happen.

WATCH CONDENSATION

1 Breathe onto the surface of a cold mirror and watch what happens.

Result: When your warm breath meets the cold mirror, water vapor in your breath condenses to form small water droplets on the surface of the mirror.

Clouds

On average, half the sky all over the world is covered with clouds at any one time. Clouds appear when moist air rises and cools down. As the water vapor in the air cools, it condenses on specks of dust in the air, forming tiny droplets of water or ice. These droplets are so small and light that they float in the air like steam coming from a kettle.

▷ *This model shows how warm air rises and cools, and how water vapor condenses to form a cloud.*

⌂ Air and humidity

There are three main reasons why air rises. First, the ground may heat the air and make it rise. Second, air rises along weather **fronts** (see pages 30-31). And finally, air may be forced up over mountains. A cloud's height depends on how much moisture, or **humidity**, is in the air. Clouds are lower when there is more humidity.

2 Warm air cools down.

3 Water vapor condenses to form clouds.

1 Warm ground heats the air, making it rise.

MEASURE HUMIDITY

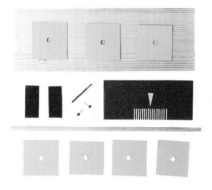

You will need: a 4 inch x 12 inch (10 cm x 30 cm) wood base, two small wooden rectangles, cardboard, two push pins, a thin dowel, a matchstick, blotting paper, glue, a pencil

1 Glue the two small blocks, 1 inch (2 cm) apart at one end of the base. Glue the matchstick to the end of the dowel.

2 Make a scale by drawing equal divisions on a piece of cardboard and adding a pointer, as shown left. Fold one end of the scale and glue it to the base so that it stands upright.

3 Push a pin into each side of the dowel, a third of the way up. Slide blotting paper squares on to the end.

4 Balance the dowel on the blocks and move the squares until the matchstick lines up with the pointer.

5 Leave your humidity tester outside in a slatted box (see page 36) and see if, day by day, the pointer rises or falls.

Result: In humid conditions, the paper absorbs water and becomes heavier. This causes the needle to rise. In dry conditions, the needle falls. Are clouds lower in humid or dry weather?

▽ *Here the level of humidity has risen.*

🌧 Cloud spotting

There are three main cloud shapes: fluffy, cotton-wool clouds called cumulus (meaning heap); flat blankets of clouds called stratus (meaning layer); and thin, wispy clouds called cirrus (meaning curl of hair). Cirrus clouds are found only at high altitudes. Cumulus and stratus clouds can be found at different altitudes. Clouds that are a mixture of cumulus and stratus clouds are called stratocumulus.

🌧 All shapes and sizes

The name of a cloud can describe its shape, height, and whether it contains rain. The word 'nimbus' in the name cumulonimbus means it is a rain or snow cloud. The word 'alto-' in the cloud names altostratus and altocumulus means the clouds are at a height between 6,000 and 20,000 feet (2,000 and 5,000 meters). In the cloud name cirrostratus, the word 'cirro-' means the cloud is above 20,000 feet (5,000 meters).

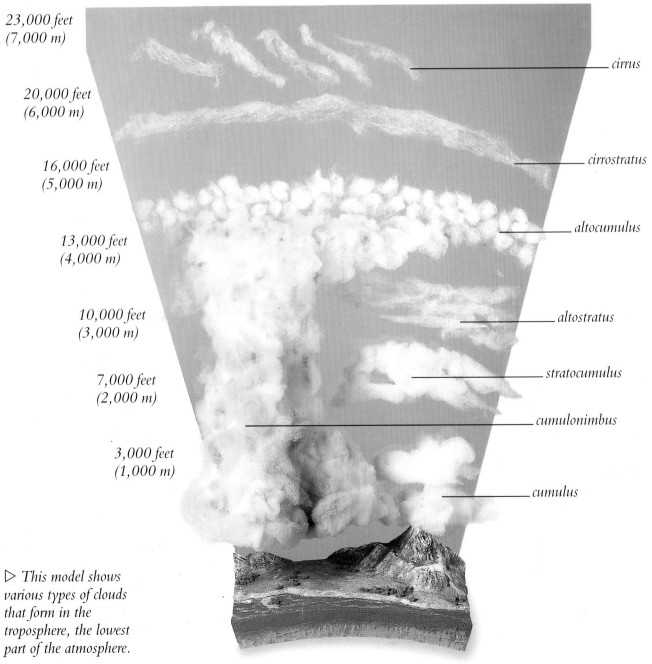

23,000 feet
(7,000 m)

20,000 feet
(6,000 m)

16,000 feet
(5,000 m)

13,000 feet
(4,000 m)

10,000 feet
(3,000 m)

7,000 feet
(2,000 m)

3,000 feet
(1,000 m)

cirrus

cirrostratus

altocumulus

altostratus

stratocumulus

cumulonimbus

cumulus

▷ *This model shows various types of clouds that form in the troposphere, the lowest part of the atmosphere.*

Rain, snow, and hail

Water falling from clouds is called precipitation. Water may fall as rain, snow, or hail, depending on the air temperature and the type of clouds in the sky. When there are clouds in the sky, precipitation doesn't always happen. It only happens when clouds become too heavy to carry all the moisture in them. The amount of precipitation in one area can be measured using a rain gauge.

△ *Rainbows happen when sunlight shines through millions of raindrops in such a way that light is split into all its colors.*

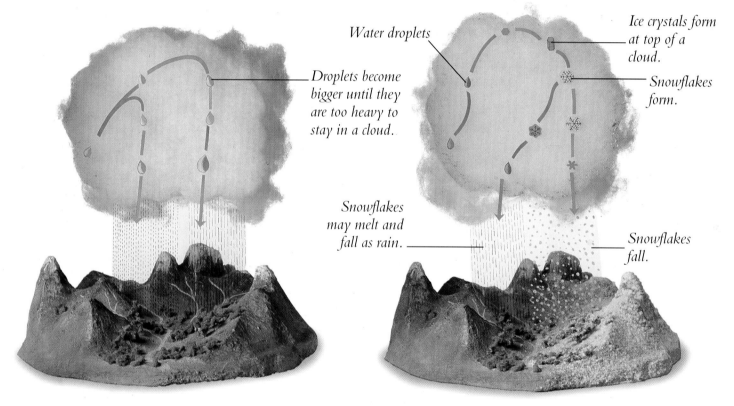

Water droplets

Droplets become bigger until they are too heavy to stay in a cloud.

Ice crystals form at top of a cloud.

Snowflakes form.

Snowflakes may melt and fall as rain.

Snowflakes fall.

△ *This cloud produces rain.*

△ *This cloud produces rain and snow.*

☔ Making rain
One way in which rain forms is by water droplets joining together. This happens in low, warm clouds. Inside these clouds, water droplets are blown about by the air. As the droplets bump into each other, they join together to make larger droplets. Eventually, they become too heavy to hang in the air and fall as rain. The longer the droplets stay in the cloud, the heavier the rain will be.

☔ Ice crystals and snowflakes
In cool areas, clouds are made up of ice crystals at the top and water droplets lower down. The ice crystals attract water droplets, which freeze on them. Many crystals stick together to make snowflakes which, when they are too heavy to hang in the air, fall out of the cloud. If the temperature rises above freezing (32 °F or 0 °C) as the snowflakes fall, they may melt and fall as rain.

MAKE A RAIN GAUGE

You will need: a plastic bottle, colored tape, scissors, a ruler, a pencil

1 Cut the top off the bottle where the curved top meets the straight sides.

2 Turn the top upside down and fit it into the base. This will stop the water inside the bottle from evaporating.

3 Cut thin strips of tape and use them to mark ¼-inch (5-mm) divisions along the straight part of the base. Pour water up to the lowest division.

4 Place your rain gauge outside, away from any buildings and trees. Record the amount of rain each day for a week, and remember to pour out the water down to the lowest division each morning.

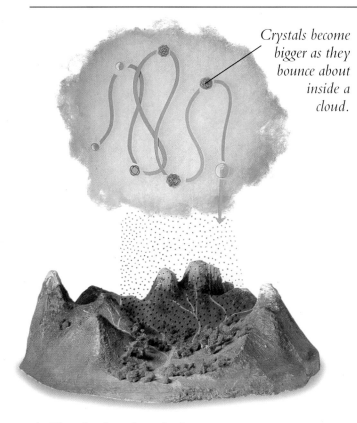

Crystals become bigger as they bounce about inside a cloud.

△ *This cloud produces hail.*

🌧 Balls of ice

Hail forms in thunderclouds when ice crystals are tossed up and down by strong currents of air. As the ice crystals are tossed up to the cold top of the cloud, the crystals attract water which freezes on them. Eventually, the crystals become too heavy to stay in the cloud and they fall to the ground as hail. Hailstones are often as big as marbles and may be bigger than tennis balls!

✏️ 🌧 Mapping precipitation

Forecasters need to know about the precipitation in a particular place to help them predict the weather. They look at the various symbols that are marked on weather maps (see page 38).

▽ *These symbols are often used on weather maps to tell us about precipitation.*

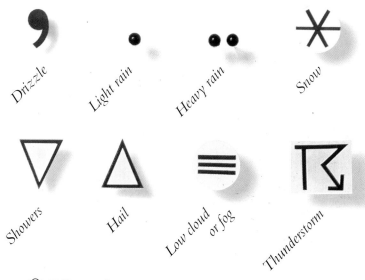

Drizzle   Light rain   Heavy rain   Snow

Showers   Hail   Low cloud or fog   Thunderstorm

🌧 Blizzards

Blizzards are snowstorms with very strong winds, low temperatures, and fine powdery snow. Wind-blown snow makes it impossible to see more than a short distance. Sometimes, people may experience *white-outs* in blizzards, when they cannot see at all and lose all sense of direction. The wind in a blizzard may also pile the snow into huge drifts, burying cars and sides of houses.

Air masses and fronts

Air masses are enormous bodies of warm or cold air that lie above areas of land and sea. Air from these air masses is blown from one place to another by global winds. When a cold air mass meets a warm air mass, they mix very slowly along a line called a front. The weather near a front is unsettled and changeable, with clouds, rain, and storms.

▷ *This model shows the movement of a warm front being followed by a cold front. The fronts are moving from left to right.*

⚑ Why do air masses form?

In some parts of the world, such as the oceans or the middle of large **continents**, the Earth's surface is similar over huge areas. The huge air masses over these areas are hot or cold, and wet or dry, depending on the land or sea underneath. These air masses are named after the places where they form. They can be hot (tropical) or cold (polar) and may form over continents (continental) or the sea (maritime).

⚑ Air masses meet

The lines where air masses meet are called fronts because they are like the front lines of a battle zone. One air mass tries to make the other move out of the way. There are three main types of fronts: cold fronts, warm fronts, and occluded fronts.

⚑ Cold fronts

In a cold front, a cold air mass slides under a warm air mass, pushing the warm air upwards. Clouds and rain occur as the warm air rises and cools. A cold front usually follows a few hours after a warm front.

⚑ Occluded fronts

An occluded front happens when a cold front catches up with a warm front and they merge together. Occluded fronts often bring heavy rain.

Large clouds bring heavy rain.

Cold front

Cold air pushes warm air upwards.

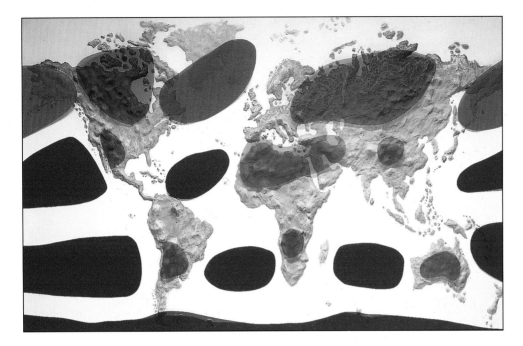

◁ *The main air masses around the world are shown on this map. The key below explains the colors shown on the map.*

■ *Continental polar: Cold and dry*

■ *Continental tropical: Hot and dry*

■ *Maritime polar: Cold and wet*

■ *Maritime tropical: Warm and wet*

Layers of clouds form.

Warm air rides up over cold air.

Cold air forced back by warm front.

Warm front

⚑ Warm fronts
In a warm front, a warm, moist air mass slides up over a cold air mass. As the warm air rises and cools, water vapor condenses to form clouds and rain. Warm air replaces cold air at ground level.

Storms

Storms are periods of bad weather that happen when huge clouds form and strong winds blow. Storms develop in different ways around the world. In temperate areas, they usually happen along fronts, where warm and cold air meet. In hot, tropical areas, storms develop because of large amounts of heat and moisture in the air.

Start of the storm

As many as 50,000 storms happen every day throughout the world. They begin when warm, moist air rises into cold air. Huge clouds build up as water vapor in the air condenses. The tops of these clouds may reach the very top of the troposphere, where the temperature is well below freezing point.

Building up energy

Inside a storm cloud, currents of air move up and down very quickly. This makes droplets and ice crystals in the cloud rub against each other, giving them an electrical charge that can be either positive or negative. Both types of charge hold energy. After a while, positive charges build up toward the top of the cloud and negative charges build up toward the bottom.

△ *These impressive lightning flashes have enough energy to light up huge sections of the night sky.*

Flashes of lightning

As the positive and negative charges in a cloud become stronger, they move toward each other. Eventually, their built-up energy is released as a flash of lightning between the two charges. The air and the ground also carry charges, so lightning can jump from clouds to the air or to the ground. Lightning heats up the air, which then expands at great speed to make the sound we call thunder.

MAKE LIGHTNING

You will need: a metal tray, a plastic sheet or cotton cloth, modeling clay, a screwdriver, a rubber glove, tape

1 Tape the sheet or cloth to a surface.

2 Adhere a ball of clay to the tray. Put on the glove and use the clay as a handle to rub the tray against the sheet or cloth for about two minutes.

3 Make sure the room is dark. With an adult's help, hold the screwdriver in your gloved hand and bring it close to the edge of the tray. Do not touch the tray with your hands.

Result: The tray builds up a charge similar to that in a storm cloud. As the energy is released to the screwdriver, you should hear a crackle and see a spark of lightning.

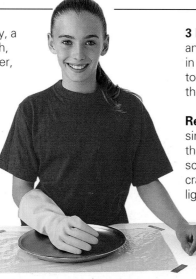
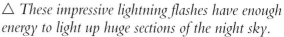

▽ *This is a model of a storm cloud, where positive and negative charges move toward each other, releasing energy as lightning.*

Lightning within cloud

Positive charge usually builds up near top of cloud ——————

Lightning strikes between two charges ——————

Negative charge usually builds up in lower parts of cloud

Lightning from cloud to air

Lightning from cloud to ground

☔ How far away?
Thunder and lightning happen at the same time. But we see lightning before we hear thunder because light travels faster than sound.

Tornadoes and hurricanes

The most violent storms of all are tornadoes and hurricanes. Tornadoes happen over land, while hurricanes develop over warm, tropical seas. Tornadoes are spinning funnels of cloud that suck up everything in their paths. A full-blown hurricane consists of torrential rain and whirling winds. Hurricanes are much larger than tornadoes. They can be 300 miles (480 km) wide, while tornadoes are no more than about 1½ miles (2.4 km) wide.

△ *The winds at the center of this tornado can reach more than 200 mph (320 kph).*

⚑ ☔ Spiraling tornadoes

Water flows quickly down a drain because it speeds up as it spirals inwards. A similar whirling motion, known as a vortex, takes place within a tornado. Tornadoes happen where warm and cold air currents meet and are always accompanied by severe thunderstorms. They are most common in the Midwest.

⚑ ☔ In a spin

Air in a tornado cloud is set spinning into a vortex by winds in the top part of the cloud. As the winds get faster, the cloud becomes shaped like a funnel. At the bottom of the cloud, more air is sucked in and the funnel reaches down to the ground. Tornadoes are strong enough to lift animals, people, and even train cars.

MAKE A VORTEX

You will need: a jug, two plastic bottles, a 20-inch (50-cm) piece of thick dowel (slightly thicker than neck of bottle), a piece of thin dowel, strong glue, scissors, modeling clay, tape

1 Stick some tape around one of the bottles, about 2 inches (5 cm) above its base. Cut off the base, using the tape as a guide.

2 Glue the necks of the bottles together. Then use tape and modeling clay to seal the joint.

3 Stand the bottles on a table and push the thick dowel into the neck, as shown left. Use the jug to fill the top bottle halfway with water.

4 With the thin dowel, stir the water around in one direction only. Now pull out the thick dowel and see what happens.

Result: The water in the top bottle spins around like the air in a tornado.

34

The life of a hurricane

1 A thunderstorm develops over the ocean.

2 Huge clouds start to form a swirl.

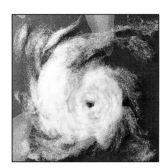

3 An "eye" forms. The storm is at its strongest.

4 The hurricane passes over land and dies out.

🏴 ☔ Hurricane winds

Hurricanes form over warm, tropical seas near the equator. In a hurricane, strong winds circle around a calm area of low pressure called the eye. As the hurricane moves, it sucks in lots of warm, moist air toward the eye. The area just around the eye has the heaviest rain and strongest gales.

▽ *In this model of a hurricane, a section has been cut away so you can see how the winds spin.*

🏴 ☔ Moving faster

Near the center of the hurricane, air spirals upwards and water vapor condenses to form huge cumulonimbus clouds. The condensation gives out heat, making the air rise even faster, sucking in more winds. When a hurricane hits land, its supply of moisture is cut off and it starts to die down.

🏴 ☔ Tracking a hurricane

Hurricanes do not move in straight lines, but they do follow similar routes. They can be tracked by satellites so people living in a hurricane's path can be warned of any approaching danger.

Air sinks slowly in eye of the storm.

Warm air spirals upwards around eye.

Rain falls from the thick clouds.

Rings of thick cumulonimbus clouds

Hurricane moves in this direction.

Direction of wind

Recording the weather

Weather forecasts predict how the weather might change. They are based on thousands of measurements of temperature, rainfall, and air pressure. With your own weather station, you can begin to make forecasts of your own.

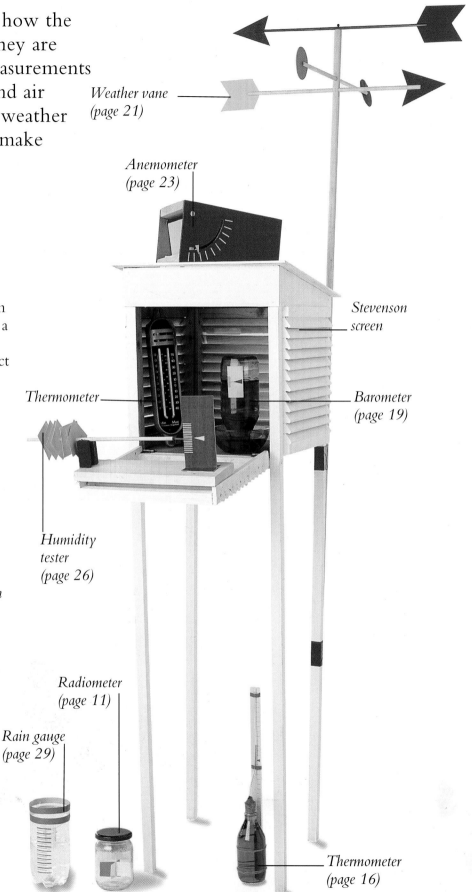

Weather vane (page 21)

Anemometer (page 23)

Stevenson screen

Thermometer

Barometer (page 19)

Humidity tester (page 26)

Radiometer (page 11)

Rain gauge (page 29)

Thermometer (page 16)

✎ Setting up
You can use the measuring instruments you have made following the directions that appeared earlier in this book, or you can buy items, such as a thermometer or a barometer, from a store. You may also want to use a box called a Stevenson screen to keep your instruments out of direct sunlight.

✎ Stevenson screens
A Stevenson screen is a raised box with slatted sides that keeps out sunlight but allows air to flow in. Its white surface reflects heat away from the instruments. If you don't have a Stevenson screen, put your instruments on a table and place a slatted wooden box over them.

▷ *Put your weather station in an open space, away from trees and buildings.*

✎ Keeping a weather record
To make weather forecasts, you need to take measurements at the same time every day, so you can compare them easily. Make a weather chart to record your measurements, as shown on the opposite page. Draw a row of columns, one for each weather feature you are measuring, such as wind speed or rainfall. Write the days when you take measurements down on one side of the chart.

MEASURE CLOUD COVER

You will need: a mirror, narrow colored tape, a pen, paper

1 With tape, divide a mirror into a grid of eight equal rectangles, as shown right.

2 Lay the mirror on the ground outside and look at the clouds reflected in the mirror.

3 The amount of sky covered by cloud is measured in oktas. Each okta means that one-eighth of the sky is covered by cloud. Add up the squares or parts of squares with cloud in them. This is the cloud cover in oktas.

▽ *These symbols are used on maps to show different amounts of cloud cover.*

○ *No clouds*

◑ *$^1/_8$ (one okta)*

◕ *$^2/_8$ (two oktas)*

◔ *$^3/_8$ (three oktas)*

◐ *$^4/_8$ (four oktas)*

⊖ *$^5/_8$ (five oktas)*

◑ *$^6/_8$ (six oktas)*

◐ *$^7/_8$ (seven oktas)*

● *Sky covered by cloud*

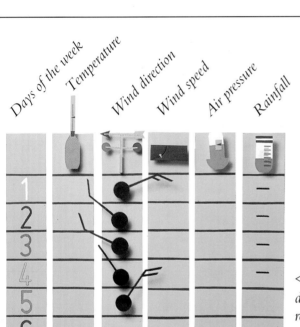

Days of the week | Temperature | Wind direction | Wind speed | Air pressure | Rainfall

▷ *Use a notebook to record your measurements.*

◁ *This chart shows daily weather recordings. You can add columns for cloud cover and humidity.*

🖋 Looking at your data

After a while, you will be able to see the pattern of the weather in your area and start using your records to make predictions. Changes in air pressure are particularly important. When the air pressure is low, is the weather wet or dry? Which direction does the wind usually blow from? If the wind direction changes, does the weather change? Are there strong winds or light winds?

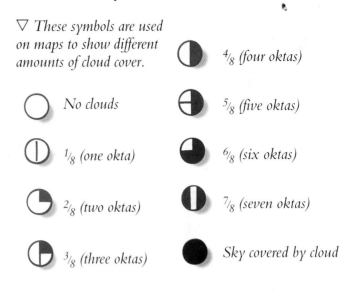

Weather maps

When meteorologists have collected their weather information, or data, they display it on maps called **synoptic charts**. These charts show weather patterns over a large area. Forecasters use these charts to see how the weather is changing and to make predictions. Some synoptic charts have small groups of numbers and symbols, called station circles, to show the measurements taken at each weather station.

▷ *This synoptic chart gives us information about air pressure and weather fronts over Western Europe.*

1024

1032

1016

| | Warm front | | Occluded front |
| | Cold front | 1023 | Isobar |

✍ Isobars and fronts

On a synoptic chart, lines called **isobars** join places with the same air pressure. Lines with spikes and bumps show weather fronts. A cold front has spikes and a warm front has bumps. An occluded front, a mixture of these two fronts, is shown by a line with both spikes and bumps.

✍ Other maps

Synoptic charts are not the only kind of weather map. Television forecasters use simpler maps with picture symbols to show features, such as rainfall or sunshine. Maps are sometimes drawn over satellite pictures to show cloud cover and the movement of winds over a large area, such as a continent.

✍ Station circles

A station circle is a group of symbols that gives information about the weather at a weather station. Look at the example to see how this information is shown. When station circles are positioned on a map, the round symbol for cloud cover marks the actual position of the weather station.

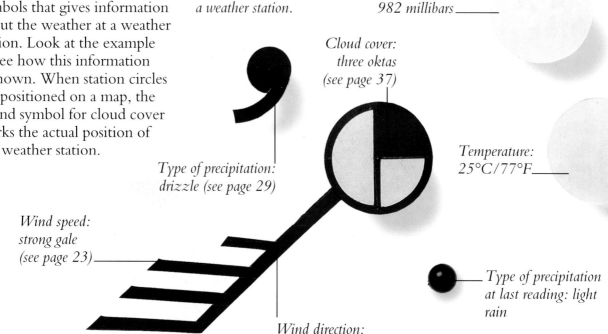

▽ *This station circle shows the reading for a weather station.*

Air pressure: 982 millibars

Cloud cover: three oktas (see page 37)

Temperature: 25°C/77°F

Type of precipitation: drizzle (see page 29)

Type of precipitation at last reading: light rain

Wind speed: strong gale (see page 23)

Wind direction: southwest

MAKE A WEATHER MAP

Before you start: Ask three friends who live near you to set up a weather station near their homes. You will need to make sure that the divisions on each instrument are the same at each weather station.

You will need: a map of your local area, pins, paper, and pens

1 Use the map of your area to mark the main features, such as rivers and towns, on a piece of paper. Mark the position of each weather station on your map.

2 Arrange with your friends to collect information from the weather stations at a particular time on a particular day.

3 After collecting all the information, use paper shapes and pins to represent it on the map. Use the symbols shown on earlier pages in this book.

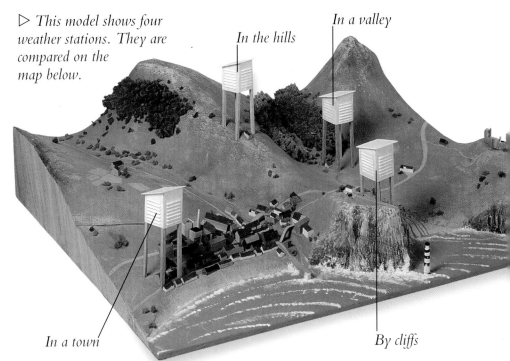

▷ *This model shows four weather stations. They are compared on the map below.*

In the hills

In a valley

In a town

By cliffs

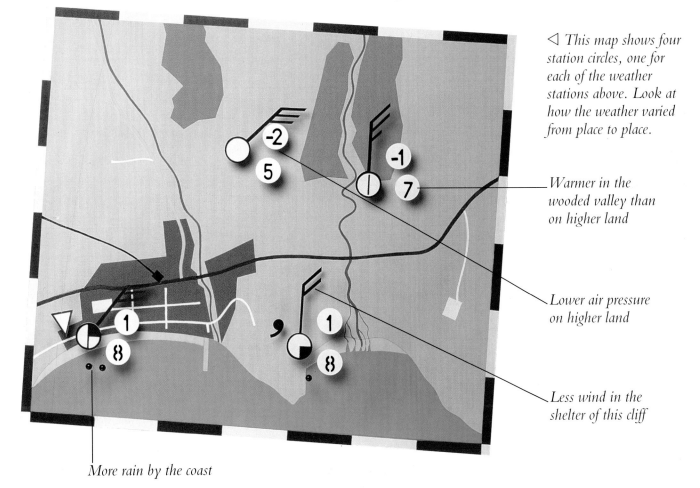

◁ *This map shows four station circles, one for each of the weather stations above. Look at how the weather varied from place to place.*

Warmer in the wooded valley than on higher land

Lower air pressure on higher land

Less wind in the shelter of this cliff

More rain by the coast

Weather forecasting

Many years ago, people predicted the weather by watching changes in nature, such as the behavior of plants and animals. Pine cones, for example, open out in dry weather to let their seeds blow away. The cones close up when rain is on the way. Today, meteorologists collect data from weather stations at sea, on land, in the air, and out in space to predict the weather.

✎ Gathering data

There are about 10,000 land weather stations around the world. At these stations, people make observations at least every three hours. At sea, ships and weather buoys take measurements and may send information to a central office via satellite. Above the Earth, aircraft and weather balloons carry instruments to measure temperature, wind speed, and air pressure.

Satellite

▽ *This model shows the main ways that forecasters gather information about the weather.*

Aircraft

Weather station

Weather balloon

Ship at sea

△ *This satellite picture shows a hurricane moving over Florida toward the Gulf of Mexico.*

✎ Weather satellites

Satellite pictures give details of the weather that cannot be seen from the ground. They show how fast clouds and fronts are moving and in what direction. There are two main types of satellites used by forecasters. Polar orbiting satellites are between 500 and 900 miles (800 and 1,400 km) above the Earth. They move around the Earth making observations over the whole planet. Geostationary satellites stay above one point on the Earth, about 22,300 miles (35,890 km) out in space. They collect information about just one area.

Weather buoy

✎ Computer power

All the weather measurements for one area are fed into a huge computer at a central weather office. The computer uses the data to work out how the weather may change in a short period of time – say 30 minutes. It then repeats this process many times until it arrives at a forecast for up to one week or 10 days ahead. During its calculations, the computer uses past records so it can take into account how weather in that area usually changes.

△ *Forecasters put together colored maps on computers to make it easier to identify weather patterns.*

✎ People and computers

Although computers are very powerful, it is the meteorologists who ultimately forecast the weather. They look at computer predictions and satellite images and use their knowledge of local conditions to make forecasts. Their forecasts are presented on television, radio, and in newspapers.

✎ How accurate are the forecasts?

Even with the help of computers, accurate forecasts can only be made up to about a week ahead. This is because the atmosphere is always changing all over the world, and what happens in one area affects what happens everywhere else. Accurate forecasts of individual showers can only be made an hour or so ahead of time.

Weather and the land

Weather and climate have an important effect on the shape of the land. Wind, rain, ice, and heat all help to break up the rocks in a process called **weathering**. Bits of weathered rock are picked up and carried away by rivers, **glaciers,** and the wind. This is called **erosion**. Eventually, the rocks are worn down and deposited in new places.

▷ *The wind and the rain have carved these desert rocks into remarkable shapes.*

🏔 Floods and landslides
When a lot of rain falls in a short time, the soil cannot soak up the water fast enough. Water collects on the surface and rivers burst their banks, causing floods. A flood can make large masses of soil and rock slide quickly downhill in mudflows or landslides. If a landslide happens on a steep slope, it can bury roads, buildings, and villages.

▷ *This model shows a landslide caused by heavy rain.*

🏔 Erosion in deserts
In some deserts, many rocky landscapes were shaped by water when the climate was wetter. Now, in dry climates, wind, heat, and gases from the atmosphere weather the rocks. Winds can easily blow away pieces of weathered rock because there are few plants to slow down the wind and hold the dry, light soil in place.

🏔 🌧 Acid rain
Sometimes, rain contains chemicals that damage buildings and forests. This is called acid rain. It forms when polluting gases from cars and factories mix with water in the atmosphere. Acid rain has killed entire fish populations in a number of lakes. High concentrations can also harm forests and soil.

Landslides often create huge steps along hillsides.

⛰ Cracking ice

In cold, wet places, such as mountains in temperate areas, water seeps into cracks in rocks and freezes at night. Ice takes up more space than water, so it pushes against the rock, forcing the cracks wider apart. During the day, when it is warmer, the ice thaws and becomes water, only to freeze again if it gets colder. Eventually, bits of the rock may fall off. This causes piles of broken rocks called scree to gather at the foot of rocky cliffs.

▽ *This model shows a mountain slope that has been shaped by the action of water freezing and thawing.*

Mountain tops shatter into jagged peaks.

Scree

Large rocks roll to the foot of the slope.

Cracks in rock face

TEST ICE POWER

You will need: an egg, a bowl, modeling clay, colored water, a freezer, a wooden skewer

1 Tap the top of the egg gently on a table and pick away the shell to make a ½-inch (1-cm) hole.

2 To empty the egg, poke a skewer into the hole and burst the yolk. Then shake the yolk and white out into a small bowl.

3 Fill the egg up to the brim with colored water. Plug up the hole with a small piece of modeling clay. Now stand the egg in the freezer for about three hours.

Result: When water freezes, it expands with such force that the egg cracks. This is the same power that forces rocks to break off cliffs as they freeze and thaw.

The changing climate

The Earth's climate has been changing for millions of years. We don't have much evidence of these changes, but we do know that the Earth has had many freezing **ice ages**. The last one ended about 10,000 years ago. Now, the Earth's climate may be warming up because people are polluting the atmosphere.

△ *By looking at tree rings, you can investigate the climate of many years ago. Narrow rings mean a year of cool, dry weather. Wide rings mean warm, wet weather.*

🏔 Looking at the past

People have kept accurate weather records for about 150 years. To look further back in time, geographers use natural records, such as **fossils** or tree rings. By looking at fossils, geographers can study the creatures that lived long ago. They work out the type of climate needed for the creatures to survive. In temperate areas, the size of growth rings in tree trunks also tells us about past climate.

🏔 Why does climate change?

Climate is affected by the Earth moving in space. If, for example, the Earth's path around the sun changes, our climate may warm up or cool down. Natural activity on the Earth's surface also affects our climate. Volcanoes sometimes form clouds of ash that stop some of the sun's energy reaching the Earth. This makes parts of the Earth cool down.

🎻 The greenhouse effect

Gases that occur naturally in the atmosphere, such as carbon dioxide and water vapor, trap heat and reflect it back to the Earth's surface. This is known as the greenhouse effect, because the gases act like the glass of a greenhouse – letting in sunlight but stopping heat from escaping. Cars, ships, factories, and burning forests release more of these gases into the atmosphere. This changes the natural balance of heat in the atmosphere and may be making the Earth warm up.

▽ *This model shows the many ways in which we pollute the atmosphere with greenhouse gases.*

Sunlight heating up the Earth

Aircraft trails contain water vapor that reflects heat.

Fumes from ships

☥ Global warming

At the moment, temperatures around the world seem to be rising by a part of a degree each year. This is called global warming. If temperatures keep rising, the middle of large continents, such as North America, may dry out during the next century, making it difficult to grow crops on the land. Water expands when it warms up, so sea levels may rise. This could flood coastal areas. Some countries are trying to reduce the amount of pollution so that global warming slows down.

△ This volcano in Alaska sends clouds of ash into the sky, blotting out the sun for long periods of time.

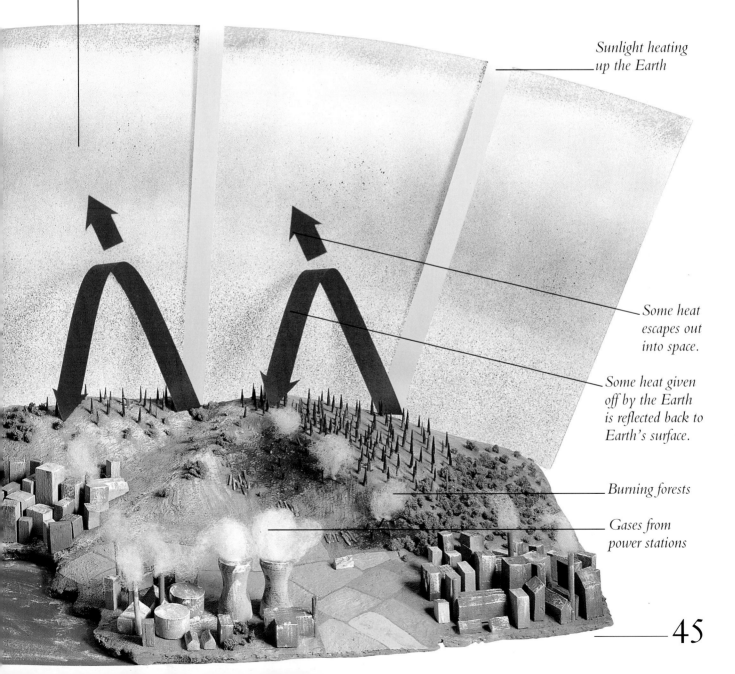

Greenhouse gases in lower atmosphere trap Earth's heat.

Sunlight heating up the Earth

Some heat escapes out into space.

Some heat given off by the Earth is reflected back to Earth's surface.

Burning forests

Gases from power stations

45

Glossary

Anemometer An instrument used to measure the speed of the wind.

Atmosphere The air that surrounds the Earth. It is made mainly of nitrogen and oxygen gases.

Barometer An instrument used to measure air pressure.

Climate The pattern of weather for a place. The climate is similar from year to year.

Condensation The process by which a gas changes into a liquid when it cools down. For example, water vapor turns into liquid water when it cools down.

Continent One of the seven large land masses of the world. The continents are: Africa, Asia, Antarctica, Australia, Europe, North America, and South America.

Coriolis effect The way that the spin of the Earth makes the world's winds bend. They bend to the right in the Northern Hemisphere and to the left in the Southern Hemisphere.

Energy The power to make things happen. The sun releases two forms of energy: light rays and heat rays.

Equator An imaginary line equal distance from each pole, which runs around the middle of the Earth, dividing it into two equal halves.

Erosion Wearing away of the Earth's surface by wind, ice, and water.

Evaporation The process by which a liquid changes into a vapor or a gas when it is heated. For example, liquid water becomes water vapor when it is heated.

Fossil The hardened remains of either a plant or animal that lived long ago. By looking at the creatures that lived in the past, geographers can determine what the climate was like thousands of years ago.

Front The boundary between two air masses with different temperatures. There are three types of weather fronts: warm, cold, and a mixture of the two called an occluded front. All fronts tend to bring rain.

Glacier A large mass of ice that forms on a mountainside when snow is packed down hard in a hollow and flows slowly downhill.

Hemisphere One half of a sphere. The equator divides the Earth into two halves: the Northern Hemisphere and the Southern Hemisphere.

Humidity The amount of water vapor or moisture in the air.

Hurricane A violent tropical storm with heavy rain, strong winds and thunderclouds swirling around a calm "eye." These storms form over warm seas near the equator. A hurricane is also called a typhoon or a tropical cyclone.

Ice age A period of very cold climate when ice covers large areas of the Earth's surface. In the past, there have been several ice ages. The last one ended about 10,000 years ago.

Isobar A line on a weather map that joins points with the same air pressure.

Meteorologist A geographer who studies the atmosphere and the weather. The word comes from the Greek word *meteoron* meaning *phenomenon in the sky*.

Monsoon A wind that draws warm, wet air from an ocean onto a continent causing a rainy season.

Ozone A form of oxygen gas. A layer of ozone in the atmosphere absorbs most of the harmful rays from the sun, preventing them from reaching the Earth.

Poles The points at the top and bottom of the Earth. The North Pole is in the Arctic and the South Pole is in Antarctica. The polar climate is very cold and dry all year around.

Precipitation Water that falls from clouds to the ground. It may be in the form of rain, hail, or snow, depending on the temperature.

Satellite A machine in space that moves around the Earth. Pictures and measurements from satellites help meteorologists to forecast the weather.

Seasons Changes in the weather throughout the year. Seasons are caused by the Earth leaning at an angle as it moves around the sun.

Subtropical climate A warm climate that is cooler than the tropics but warmer than temperate areas.

Synoptic chart A weather chart drawn using observations made at the same time in different places. Synoptic means *seen together*.

Temperate climate Mild, rainy climate of places that are neither too hot, nor too cold. These places are between the hot tropics and the cold poles.

Temperature How hot or cold something is.

Thermometer An instrument used to measure temperature. Most thermometers measure temperature in degrees Fahrenheit (°F) and degrees Celsius (°C).

Tornado A violent whirlwind that extends from a cumulo-nimbus cloud to the ground.

Tropical climate Hot climate of places close to the equator. Tropical climates may be wet all year around or have wet and dry seasons.

Troposphere The lowest layer of the atmosphere, nearest the ground, where the weather happens.

Water vapor Water in the form of a gas in the atmosphere.

Weathering The process by which rock is broken up into soil and sand by heat, water, ice, plants, or chemicals.

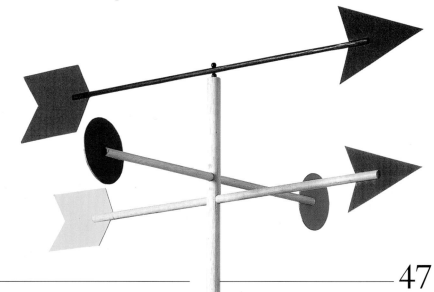

Index